F.J. Williams

The Model Shop

For Kai
and Gary
with every good wish
from John Williams
Christmas 2012

First published in 2011
by Waterloo Press (Hove)
95 Wick Hall
Furze Hill
Hove BN3 1NG

Printed in Palatino by
One Digital
54 Hollingdean Road
East Sussex BN2 4AA

A CIP record for this book is available
from the British Library

ISBN 978-1-906742-35-5

Acknowledgements

Thanks are due to the editors of the following publications in which some of my work has previously appeared:

Agenda, Black Rose, Borderlines, Envoi, Equinox, The Leopard, Lines On The Map, Oracle, Pen Pusher, Planet, Raw Edge, The Rialto, Seventh Quarry and *Thalassa.*

By the same author

Reading Lesson in the Lifers' Wing (Peterloo Poets, 2009)
Grammar Matters (with M. Ross; Pearson International, 2006)
Ways With Plays (with D. White; Carel Press
Contribution to *Key Thinkers in Linguistics and Philosophy of Language* (Edinbugh University Press)
Papers in the *Transactions of the Lancashire and Cheshire Historical Society*

Contents

I: *The Model Shop*

II: *The Rain Gauge*

for Elsie and Mavis

I
The Model Shop

The Model Shop

We've lived in a lot of previous lives
Falling in love, new ways to flourish,
The discipline of Empire and the polished court.
This time, small folk in packets, freeze-dried trees,
A bag of bus-stops, instant ivy
The smell of toyshop varnish.
No-one recalls the agreed way of hope,
How we put the landscape together,
The cardboard hills and ready-made rubble
Into its slow explosion.
For those with the whole day off,
God repeats himself in the flat-pack doll's house,
The rubber furniture and plastic piano
Hushed of all arpeggios,
Rules for remembering the future.

Working in the Crack-Up Room

All day in Building Ten it's been big picture talk,
The nine-day week, the ten-task job,
Great ideas for the next big thing,
Younger, leaner, all drawn in.
We leave the focused market for the crack-up room,
The Clinton suit and Straight Inc. ties.
Success dissolving body from the mind
In buzz-group graphs and short-term gain.
We disappear. All flesh is grass.
We're like the freezing water in the glass.

Busy time on Brash Street

The braless, liberated co-eds
Return from sushi lunches, dimsum bars and
Compact mirrors where the other mind resides
To deal on paper, small print, phone and screen
That smoothes out wrinkles with the glow
Of steady purpose.
Watching them swing round
The edge of extinction from their black-ice teas,
They've killed the angel in the house
To answer the line of beauty.
So troubled with lashes,
A few piercings and heavy eyes,
What time would it be where they come from?
Eight hours at the dream machine
A ghost looks back from the targets and agendas
Calling to account an edgy talent
Heading for the shredder.
So who's to blame in this world of top-floor
Offices where the boss resides in franchise
And different history?
Four minutes to live. They return from busy time,
Stiff briefcases at the hip,
Glancing at watches white and hard,
Pleating uniforms to play in the burning wreckage.

Cashpoints

By day they stand with the Chocolate Machines,
strong and sturdy in a pillar of tiny bricks
yearning for darkness when they illuminate
the car park with the yellow glare of the bank account.
We touch them in the face, press close and stare
at their reminders of immortal energy
among the idling engines and reversing lights,
with others who attend and mark in verse
a different progress through the universe.

Depression furniture

They made you cold no matter how you sat,
those no-designer chairs bought before the war
for front rooms and special company.
A touch on the heavy side,
made of planks and bed springs,
and nailed in the warehouse with joiners' cloth.
You saw the world sitting in a suitcase.
But it was a special occasion just the same;
we'd sit for a bit then climb the stairs
through the chilly house to see grandma
with her free specks and view of the by-pass,
as if she'd come with coupons too,
her bed hammered together around her like a tea-chest:
and something gone away, quietly gone away,
slow to let our hands go, mourn the loss of mind.

The glass blower

Six floors of tyre and rubber factory
rise above the shed where he sits astride
a black tin-box splattered with pink and blue
drawing a kind of wonder out of the zig-zag
lines of glass, blow-torch, hand-irons, tongues
tensed to hold a chandelier, flower or fish:
lifting his head to see the glossy bronze die
into a frail wick of metaphor that we see by.

The Prison Band

Ideally you should be on your own
in row Z uncorking the cognac
to expand the map,
but Tiger and the Jewellery Men
start up like a lorry with bad gears
closing down the eight-ball,
switching off the doughnuts
and finishing with a lonely F
from the half-ton piano.

The cuts are starting to bite
as we put away Fat Chicks and everyone's silent
in the glassed-in room that sounds of jazz.
Next door must be alright,
stewing for years, tidying up on Friday
for the Shadow Show with their bottles
in the Blokes' room,
it's the cult of one, the sky using the sea to weep.

An ounce of Mersey beach glass

After years coming this way
to tell how some small pleasure died
these chips of bottle and blue computer screen
return in a tangle of sea hair with their own sparse stories;
the neck of a bottle of scent, shards of windscreen
and crushed spectacle scattered in a terrible dispersal:
intact knick-knacks of Late and Early china
as if we like to see ourselves as less,
in a maker's mark, in a bristle of glass
snapped off deep in the thumb,
or the sea cutting fresh glass from an orchid vase
that brings whole rooms to light
and the ceiling shaken by the sea's weak hiss.

Scout Uku and the guitar class

Unpacking snapshots at the bottom of the box
we come across Scout Uku and the guitar class
gently asserting themselves with go-to-hell guitars.
Even now the scene assembles their bright blue pants,
nickel-coloured hair, flip-flops, hats
and barely a wrinkle of blue.
They play their chords tuned to low D
in sensibly buckled chinstraps
and settle in the rope-house
with their second-hand guitars
moving in and out of focus
to prove the secret order of the world
that burns and freezes inside their buried box
and slips away to a cool white sheet.

Parker's Guide to Cars

Past beauty and the erotica mags
We come to Parker's Guide to Cars
Along the shelf like big cheap postcards.
The newsagent stacks his cans,
Listens to the bulletin-breaks on the radio
And displays his choky four-wheel drives
Like big electric heaters and forbidding.
Balancing sportscars on our fingertips
We touch the two forevers, plummeting and fun.

Lost corners

We gave them over to abandoned things,
the lost corners stacked against the skirting board
with old records, magazines and papers.
One time in the shed beside the house
a bundle of slacks and jumpers
gathered in a lost corner with the broken tools
and the lawnmower we couldn't throw away,
as if grief and failure came clear at last
just as mother's silvery hair tied back
for the deep green bowl where with flour
she dipped her hands a thousand times,
folding jam inside the pancakes,
into lost corners' transitory taste and splendour.

Disaster Team

Failing rehab, we join the Disaster Team;
a fire of hoola-hoops and cans of foam,
big bright flashes of artificial people
packaged in wraparound reflector specs.
We press together in the imaginary flood,
different bits of life laid across the car park;
the girl-scout prayer, a traffic-kiosk,
a big blue light like an emergency,
and our big splash to vanish with the keys.

The old Dansettes

They're still for sale, the old Dansettes
The portable plywood players that skipped,
Suitcase size with stubby knobs for the sound,
Out of place among the DVDs and PC cards.
A dozen records such a luxury
And speakers that carried in the shapely box
Each album nearing the centre's six big blasts.

Old Physics

Historic, stunning and totally forgotten
the old physics with its Exploded Views
and electric jam jars, everything ending up
in the sink. Before theme pubs,
mail order jackets and rubber fetish bras
old science trained with torches
and wrong-size batteries for the hi-tech boom.
Crumbs, we thought, watching Neil and Buzz
and Hazel Rogers opposite working her red ponytail
round and round her finger, reaching question 5,
before the dead possessed us or we carried their genes.

Aunt's

She kept the sepia oval portrait of the family
Bleaching us to the hue of ancient newspaper
In the room she never used
Except to write in curly pen
Among the air that smelt of foliage.
Sometimes when she dozed off
I sat in her kitchen with a bottle of wine
Taking a look at her Mr Universe magazines
She clustered in her dresser with the cheval glass.
Now it's May, she's coming out of the coma
So we're back and forth in the taxi
And reduced to a hairpin from the vanity box,
The dusty gleam of temporary wealth.

Trip to the Amnesia Clinic

I change round the bread bin and the biscuit tin
and wait for my son's six lines of handwriting
for his little school before I rest on the table
and scrub two more things from the must-do list.
Our carpet's full of moths rubbed off the page
to restore the blankness he spoiled with each sentence.
The paraffin stove drawn with a face
blunts the misery of January,
prophet-faced, wise and passing the test.

Woolworths

As if we've followed the wrong god out of church
With hankies, gift mugs and paper flags,
We find we're on the other side of sacrifice

And everything's to celebrate:
The music of doo-wop coaxing time back
And the smell of peppermint balls and leather.

Say you came here the first muddy days of March
For power cream and wow pans
To prepare the weekend break

With garden lamps that burn all year like shrines
Or glad in August to be out of the sun
With the beach bags, ball and sandals,

You'll build a boat like a long golden answer
To find what matters, chance or time.
Or maybe it's a frozen afternoon in October,

Elvis singing to help you notice the wild
Bird feeders, the coils of wire,
Autumn made of last moments.

Or attracted by the Christmas lights
You'll remain and feel a future taking shape,
Happy to stand in the striplights and be counted.

Car Parts Store

Setback for mavericks behind the builder's yard,
the world has come to bits in trays of screws,
old cars broken down and dismantled
from construction sites and sorting bays;
sixty thousand parts in Keep Wrap cellophane
as if you'd wrapped the air and given it out
greasy and gray with the You Had Me calendar.
It's a place for mending the mind
after sitting in the jams of the Keep Clear zone
with no memory but a tyre chart
and shiny signs about customer care.
Some bolder vision might make us seek
the bones of laughter among the broken engines
and dead headlamps of the two-bob tram;
a new Master of the Universe perhaps
or the last death in the velvet jail.

The Oracle Corporation

They know where to sit to untangle the harps
The ghost boys in the Oracle Corporation.
Given a choice they'd be born invisible
Openers of worlds previously unremarked.
While in Geranium City it's talk of pills
And the three-way world, the shape-up scheme
In springy gutters and tears at the water fountain.
Tuesday, it's the happiness patrol
With Kyoto Gas and climate change;
Hanging round the shopping centre,
Blaring our horns in different honks,
Warning, friendship, lust.

The Fish Van

The boss, flesh-faced in bottle-lens specs,
two coats and leggings for the frozen fish,
with big knives and buckets for the floor,
crammed ten deep with the sea cod;
we worked from the back of the van,
door-to-door as far as the big estates,
from the ploughed-up football field to the farms.

I pushed back the door to a cloud of steam,
cold coins, crumpled bills and our words
on the doorstep pale for the fish we sold;
cod, haddock, monkfish, trout,
the thud of each fish on the frozen wall of the van,
and the man who convinced us he was dead.

The Jug Stall

I learnt to smoke at Bible camp, under the jug stall,
after the goodnight potatoes with a pack of Park Drive
from the machine two stops out in Coca-Cola land.

The Truth band played 'Anthems for Africa'
and the Warden wanted the music down
for the 'Balm of Gilead' at lights out.

We crouched in the call-to-holiness position,
lighting the grains of fire under the jug stall
to taste the bars and restaurants of Hollywood

while the camp around us slept with pledges.
Next day we sprayed Kenya on the map in aerosol,
posing for a picture on the Zulu rope bridge,

on either arm, a companion from the jug stall,
pockets filled with cigarettes for the life ahead,
aim, apparatus, method and score.

Area 44

Nearly new and going to hell,
My first guitar behind the counter
In Sam's Same Day Turnaround
Where we played with flames licking our feet
On mounds of cracked plums and dried peas.
Once we played in the hat room
To his father's standard Co-op casket
On a half-foot of shelf space
And the ominous effect of gauze.
We thought ka-boom
The part of the brain that recognises melodies
And climbs up to the window on a steamy range
Of rubbish to behold the guitars,
The standard narrow face, straightened hair,
Buddy, Elvis and the suitcases of doom.

From the Gallery

The history choir is asleep on the grass
with picnic packs and ice-cream tubs,
saucers and impressions in the field.
Someone puts off shoes and opens Chloe Jealous
as the five-minute bell rings to gather scores,
take chairs upstairs with the sunlit brass.
Memories don't care where they live,
the beginner's orchestra, the history choir,
a far-off ignition turning over that cannot catch.

Misprint in last year's horoscope

Miss Kinkyboots has been at it again,
with old style stand-by-your-man
and crap about a love affair:
find that glimpse and you'll see a Leo.
It should have read don't.
Five pubs, two bars and a nightclub later
it's survival time at the Casablanca,
beef Wellington and firm pears
under a leaky roof with no jazz.
Sitting it out 's like history taking a break
in Velcro, teabags and tetrapak.
That's how we leave the world,
outside Kenyon's clothes shop skint;
all the Leos and losers, and more last words.

Replicas

When you've had enough of roads
and lived three lives searching for diners,
lookalike homes and walked with bursting luggage
and your grey suit on a hanger,
hesitating at the lights like a huge sweep of sadness,
you remember the replicas:
the fake breasts, a radio clock,
a miniature golf ball chewing-gum machine
with its plastic animals shedding old layers
down to some imagined core:
and hear the girls in harpy night gowns
driving half the night and pulling in at eight.

The smoking room

Six floors you climb to the smoking room,
past Mr Wax and the Kookai Club,
miniaturised amazements in Love and Laugh
with their dayglo wigs and Groucho specs.
You'd think there'd be some revelation
after climbing six floors: a surge of prickly fire
or a girl-band leaning against the rail.
But here you stand with crinkly ash trays,
banging of the steel door in the heartless striplights,
your brain map all aglow
to find among the smoking room body, mind and soul.

Pinball Machines

There's never any time in the amusement park
For the big machines and the pinball games,
The extra shots and high score red and greens
In the chilling giggle of pinball art.
A whole past banging around
Among the balls like lost pieces of time
Without a moment for us in the extra night.
The best spend their lives in here
In the loosely joined new centuries
And score ten thousand million in the dark.

Lunch-time flat

Browsing for a tyre-place with my lunch-time flat,
gate after gate of scrapped iron and reborn cars
on the noisy ring road into town,
I reach The Silence Company up ahead.
Grateful for its stacked exhausts and roadside ads,
I greet the mechanic among his Astras and Corsaires,
with his wheel-gun sucking and whining for tyres,
and I explain the blow-out in the door-shaped sun,
the lunch-time toaster glowing in the back
with the tacked-up Klimt and Michelin man,
Harley, Harley beats the test of time,
in the three-way world of rubber, glass and can.

Mr Sullivan

This one's for you, Mr Sullivan, who made it clear
the first freezing weeks of 'sixty eight
running our class casino wasn't for you
in your small glittery glasses and wheezy blowing.
We were going places, helping at the service station,
clawing through rubbish for Coca-Cola bottles,
mopping aisles of drink at Nate and Als'
and giving out leaflets for Maybelline.
You socked a few dingers for history
with captured Whermacht maps and paper countries,
flashing into simplicity and powerless to be born.

The Framer's

We bring our birthday photos, dogs and cars
to his low bulbs, set squares, knives and saws.
I've driven past a thousand times
watching his frames, the open case of instruments,
walnut, lime and oak give way to plastic and veneer.
I'd like to watch him peering into his workbench
where the Taj Mahal of ring-pulls, an embroidered bird
or someone's sketch from life
taxes his interpretation of the world,
his wall of glazes, mounts and frames,
the golden wedding fat within its frame.

II
The Rain Gauge

White Mulberry

In case we overdose and nearly die
we need to grow some on our bit of porch,
a couple of pots or in a flower-box.
It's the antidote to poison, to bad blood,
the White Mulberry and glamorous catapult
releasing pollen at half the speed of sound,
nothing faster in the living world.
Physics can name the force inside the catkin,
hemmed in, the jostle of captivity.
If Hades had a website, we'd see it there,
the berry, the white leaves and the addicts
with their fire alarms, pink skies of arson,
stolen motorbikes and earthquakes.

Card school in the boiler-room

Others are not so lucky, driving round after work,
looking for bands to see and parties to crash,
or those who love their jobs and then go home.
But in the corner of the boiler room
we keep our poker school, creeping across
mops and rusty spanners, scraping iron chairs
and shuffling on a bucket beneath the anglepoise.

O Fortuna, your hands are like a sunset,
let me know when to fake and when to fold.

We play by ear, listening for an ace
in the squeak of a shoe or a catch of breath,
a royal flush in someone's itchy eye;
everything speaks through something else,
like the lit centre, gathering us
in the pared-down prose of a poker game
that sends us home smelling of luck and cinders.

Heavy users

Brain imaging illustrates in colour
what must be going on inside our heads
on hearing good news, sitting in a jam
or taking off our clothes before we love.
Now they've located the physical seat
of human passions down to swarms of blue
at last we see the light that guides the heart.

But not everyone wielding a test-tube
walks from night to morning, seeing clearly
through the gas cloud. Take the heavy users,
or those so cold no fire can warm their heart,
or he to whom the animals and plants
betrayed their secrets, on the verge of tears,
Darwin who kept it quiet for twenty years.

The gas bill

Stepping over the gas-bill at my front door,
I smell the frozen dinner baking from Bargain Box
and hear a whole Woman's Hour devoted to peppers.
The D-shaped meal pings, tasting
like a message dropped through the door;
the briefest card from the bank,
an advert from Warm Windows,
a clutch of free bin-bags,
peanuts from the gas god
with his sky-high bills
and pipes beneath the road,
whose gift of final spasm is our silence.

The whoosh

Swiped from a car, a radio needs the freezer;
nestling in the ice-box, the key code breaks
and you switch it on, the brilliance unimpaired.
Too little's been said about the sound
as things erase from history; secret codes,
car number plates that drop from sight,
a re-sprayed motorbike running round town
or things chucked away like bendy wire
for breaking into vans, the Styrofoam coffee cups
that listen through a wall
at the bodiless voices of the neighbours.
Think of the hairgrip that never lets you down;
the tiny click, a brief god opening a Chubb,
and that collection, a freezer full of radios
among the luncheon meat and tomatoes,
the high-amp socket that restores the whoosh.

Directory Enquiries

Fishing around in the address book
for a number I can't find, I dial Directory.
Three rings, then Edelweise comes down the line.
Everyone is hanging on for opening hours,
train departures, the yellow page of dreams.
Hard to name the art: the muse of clicks,
the staff directory, a city of ghosts
moving sentences among the Edelweise.
I envy them phoning from Miami,
advancing on string-and-tin, drum and smoke
meeting at the end of opposed winds.
Now it's Jesu Joy in plinks. I say
I hope I miss the Cradle Song this time
just as the operator speaks…

The wigwam speech

Scissored from a trucker magazine
full of gimme hats and belt-buckle ads,
the picture of the wigwam we constructed
out of doors with floor mats and four garden canes.

It was those wrestling, hugging ages, seven to ten
when we had to make a totem pole
and talk in wigwam speech,
ker-epa-nai-zha and nap-chin-a-wink,
dragging the stove out of the greenhouse
into the wigwam with anything that burned.
It felt like sitting in a cupboard with the cramps,
your heart the beating map of America,
talking wigwam in my arm-wrestler's jacket
and the peace pipe hissing with its ash.

The Funfair winter depot

Walking between the frozen booths
with the toxic tang of diesel
I notice the frosty edge of everything;
the pink and yellow sideshows,
the wheel-assemblies, powered steering
and the trailers of banished gods
who relied on doo-wap and shimmy-shimmy
instead of hymns, their big words collapsing
like the introverted Ghost House that sticks
in the mind all your life and the Death Ride
with its hot sin, perished tyres and popcorn,
making hell smell sweet and our frozen lives
for the god of love who requires that we should die.

Befriending the receptionist

So I can cover my ass, I befriend the receptionist,
for love like hate is always acted out.
I bring her the fizz to cure all thirsts
and a rose for her hard little heart,
showing an interest in her Guy mags
and showbiz birthday charts.

I chase her street shoes and her office shoes
round the squat little letters of her desktop
where she welcomes the mad and specialist,
deals with the screech of messages in purgatory
and squeezes my hot balls
of paper in her hand.

Punching in and out of work each day
in the toxic sludge of the small print,
I'm lucky to have so much to lose
as I sag on the ropes from the fight;
her body scarcely moves to save my ass
and washes down her sandwich with my Sprite.

The night packers

Stuck in the tube with the famous four guitar chords
beating through the vents, I brace in the queue
with a couple of night packers made handsome
in their plastic jackets, and a trace of sneer
and bitch about the boss and punishing
schedule at Millie's Open Late
where they squeeze parsnips into carrier bags
and the canteen shuts at four.

I overhear… what he said and what I said
and what does she know one pay packet
away from homelessness?
Then the train takes a jolt and the lights go off
and we're on the scary hymns.

But the packers continue: sorting out the plastics,
who's in the freezer, who's in the oven,
their outlines appearing in the emergency light
and their snap tins glinting by their knees
from the life we require elsewhere.
What would we leave from our long list of jobs
these few moments stuck in the dark,
with the problem of the trolley in the yard?

Taps

They stare downcast into the kitchen sink,
waiting for their next part to appear,
briefly colouring at a cup or tomato
and the forty watts wasting in the stairwell.
They'll fill pans and wash bowls,
comparing us with the u-bend and water tank,
waiting to wash our day face and night face
into the plastic drain,
envying the fridge its floodlit trays,
the orange buzz of the electric fire,
the lock its twiddle as we turn the key.

Hats

All of us wear several hats; the office,
workshop or classroom, burning the punch-clock,
the automatic eye that lets us in
and out; the red hat for the overdraft,
the black for vigilance, for sobriety.

This is the one I wear, high on thinners
and squirts of glue, cutting out the ocean
with kindergarten scissors, scraping gunk
that'll never come off the furniture.
I have another two for the camera,

the Saturday hat and the Sunday hat,
at home with long spiels from the radio,
where scientists say how gravity's weak;
metals were liquid; we came from the sun,
the unforgettable kinks of logic.

There are hats that listen and those that speak,
sing, dance and die among our relentless
standards. The politician's hat, a flag
on the skinny pole of belief; the queen's
whose headdress of bronze they dug from a pit.

Pavement drinks

Among God's liquids we find the pavement drinks;
street restaurants serving coffee in tinted cups
and tea, that sea of healing among the pots and jugs.
Like in the cave at Delphi, wine splashed out
onto the table, onto the floor
searches for form and shatters the sun
into a thousand lights.
There's a dish of olives prismatic with oil
and a scoop of cream beseeching you to stay
among the flavours and vinegar bottles
with their bitter interpretation
so we might understand heaven at last.

Gismos

Just when you thought it worth travelling to earth,
six floor of parking and everyone feasting at Franks,
they changed the way we fall in love
to diverts, call-backs and answer machines.
Now we need a phone, a tiny piece of death
and a voice like speech from the oxygen tent
as if we've overdosed on pills or weed.

There are clicks, pings, sounds of outer space,
another self landing with whisks and timers,
gismos with a little shred of heart
pretending to love us so we star their names,
the comfortable crash of disbelief.

The car park man

High up on the how-to-have-fun list
comes the car park man allowing us in
and out of work with the barrier button.
He uses up his time with the big green go light,
tasting chewed pencils and bringing us to book.

Five hundred cars-a-day tremble past his kiosk,
enamel surfaces nicked and keyed
from the city and the building-site:
early birds and night owls stacked and locked
with conference files, week-end bags and tennis balls.

His gift for broad address,
his uh-huh handed down from heaven
like a distant squall of rain.
One last day, which would he choose
with his squared and dotty paper checking us in;
the stream of dripping cars and the webcam
or the multi-storey's life-guide for the stressed?

Rain gauge

My father came down every morning
to make the fire and tap the glass,
scrape up coal and open the paper
to draw flame, then step into the yard
to take advice from the sky.

Strike a match for his Golden Virginia
where he'd tap the rain gauge put together out of a shot-
glass and joiner's rule
and coax down the stubborn tears of night.

He kept a pen just for the weather
that came for him over the house
and filled his lungs at the door,
tightening the Windsor knot at his throat,
permitting a small piece of home a history:
stripped trees, breeze rising, the Arctic bare of ice.

Hotpoint

Our clothes tumble together in the glass,
the round window of the washing-machine
where my garage shirts and your happy socks
and our bedspread thrash around till vanished,
or set to kindness, the underwired bra
holds its shape in the metal and still moves.

Then in the second cycle of shock art,
when a jumper with jellybaby arms
emerges from the dryer as Snoopy gear,
slimmed down after decades on delicate,
as if we're in an advert-break to show
the bra's missing wire, the cup sagging down
and I, like Satan at the sight of Eve,
stupidly good, of enmity disarmed
am waiting for the wardrobe on the line.